Let's Get Moving!

Contents

- Animal Action — 2
- Getting Started — 4
- Hitching a Ride — 6
- Fast Forward — 8
- Ups and Downs — 12
- The Hunters — 14
- The Hunted — 16
- Moving Together — 18
- Surprising Moves — 22
- Animal Glossary, Index — 24

Animal Action

Animals move in many different ways. Some run or hop. Others slide, swim, or fly. Sometimes animals have to take quick action to escape danger. They also need to move to find or catch food.

A HERD OF BISON

Getting Started

Some baby animals, such as elephant calves, can walk for miles almost as soon as they are born.

Other young animals need more help. For example, newborn cubs and kittens cannot move very well by themselves. When their mother wants to move them, she picks them up by the scruff of the neck and carries them.

A LIONESS AND HER CUB

Hitching a Ride

Some animal babies need to hitch a ride, usually on their mother's back. There are many reasons why baby animals do this: for safety, for speed, and sometimes just for a rest!

A mother scorpion carries her young on her back. They are protected by the fierce sting in her tail.

Arrow poison frogs carry their tadpoles to the water after they hatch. Once the tadpoles are in the water, they are able to swim by themselves.

A baby orang-utan holds onto its mother as she swings through the trees.

Fast Forward

Many animals are very fast movers. The cheetah is the fastest animal on land. The peregrine falcon and the eagle are among the fastest birds. These birds reach speeds in the air much faster than the cheetah can reach on land.

Giraffes can reach speeds of up to 32 miles per hour.

A cheetah can run as fast as 70 miles an hour. That's more than the speed limit for cars on many freeways!

Some speed comparisons

Peregrine falcon	180 miles per hour
Cheetah	70 miles per hour
Sailfish	65 miles per hour
Racehorse	45 miles per hour
Fastest human	20 miles per hour
Turtle	$1/10$ mile per hour

Ups and Downs

Some animals move in leaps and bounds. Other animals stay on the ground and move by slithering and sliding.

The kangaroo moves around by jumping. It uses its tail for balance and pushes with its powerful hind legs. Kangaroos can jump as far as 42 feet.

Snails leave a trail of sticky slime as they move. This helps them to slide along.

The sidewinder snake lives in the desert. It moves sideways, and tilts its body, so that its stomach is not burned on the hot desert sand.

Fleas are tiny insects, but they are the best jumpers in the animal kingdom. A flea can jump up to 15 inches; that's about 130 times its own length.

The Hunters

Animals that hunt have some special actions to help them catch their prey.

When wolves are hunting, they often use a slow type of running called *loping*. They can track their prey for hours, until it is too tired to keep running.

14

Crocodiles are able to move quickly through the water and snatch food with their huge jaws.

AN EAGLE SWOOPING DOWN ON ITS PREY.

The chameleon lizard stays very still when an insect approaches. Then it flicks its long tongue out for the catch! All this takes just a fraction of a second.

The Hunted

Moving can be especially important when a hunter is about! Some animals run from danger – as quickly as possible. Other animals move quickly and quietly to hide.

When baby shrews hear their mother's special "danger" signal, they line up behind her. They hold on to each other with their mouths. Then the whole line moves together to a hiding place!

A springbok deer leaps high into the air, a sign that danger is about.

When zebras are on the run, their stripes make it hard for a hunting animal to pick out one zebra from the herd.

17

Moving Together

For many kinds of animals, staying safe means staying in a large group. The animals move around together to find food. Young animals have more protection than they would have with just their parents. And when one animal in the group senses danger, the message quickly gets around.

When a beehive becomes too crowded, many of the bees leave to seek a new home. They swarm together until a new place is found.

A group of fish is called a school, or shoal.

A HERD OF WILDEBEEST

Many animals don't just move around each day to find food. They *migrate* each year from one part of the world to another, sometimes traveling thousands of miles. Some animals form large groups when the time to migrate comes around.

Many birds, such as this flock of Canada geese, migrate to warm areas during winter.

Monarch butterflies migrate in large groups or swarms.

Surprising Moves

Some animals have special moves for special situations. A hummingbird can fly from place to place, but it can also "hang" in midair to drink nectar from flowers. When it does this, its wings are actually moving very fast – too fast for our eyes to see.

The sugar glider lives in trees and is a very good climber. But it can also take to the air and glide from tree to tree.

A frill-necked lizard usually scurries along on four legs. But when it is threatened it runs on two legs, looking as fierce as possible.

Animal Glossary

ARROW POISON FROG   a frog that has sacs of poison on its skin, protecting it from attackers.

CHAMELEON   a kind of lizard from Africa that can change the color of its skin to match its surroundings.

FRILL-NECKED LIZARD   a lizard that lives in the deserts of Australia.

KANGAROO   an Australian animal which moves by hopping along on its powerful hind legs.

SAILFISH   a large fish that gets its name from its large fin, which looks just like a sail.

SPRINGBOK   a kind of antelope from Africa.

SUGAR GLIDER   a small animal that lives in trees in Australia and New Guinea.

WILDEBEEST   a large, African antelope, also called a gnu.

Index

albatross 3
arrow poison frog 7
babies 4-5, 6-7
bees 19
bison 2
chameleon 15
cheetah 8-9, 10
crocodile 15
dog 3
eagle 14-15
elephants 4
fish 2, 19
flea 13
frill-necked lizard 23

geese 20
giraffes 9
humans 10-11
hummingbird 22
hunting 14-15, 16
kangaroo 12
lions 5
migration 20-21
monarch butterflies 21
orang-utan 7
peregrine falcon 8, 10
racehorses 10-11

sailfish 10-11
scorpions 6
shrews 16
sidewinder snake 13
snail 12
springbok 17
sugar glider 23
turtle 10
wildebeest 18-19
wolves 14
zebras 16-17